iParenting Media Award Winner

Dude, That's RUDe!

(Get Some Manners)

Dude, That's RUDe!

(Get Some Manners)

by Pamela Espeland & Elizabeth Verdick

Illustrated by Steve Mark

free spirit
PUBLiSHiNG®

Helping kids
help themselves™
since 1983

Library of Congress Cataloging-in-Publication Data
Espeland, Pamela
     Dude, that's rude! : get some manners / by Pamela Espeland & Elizabeth Verdick.
          p. cm. — (Laugh & learn)
     Includes index.
     ISBN-13: 978-1-57542-233-6
     ISBN-10: 1-57542-233-6
     1. Etiquette for children and teenagers. I. Verdick, Elizabeth. II. Title.
     BJ1857.C5E87 2007
     395.1'22—dc22

                                                                 2006031531

At the time of this book's publication, all facts and figures cited are the most current available. All telephone numbers, addresses, and Web site URLs are accurate and active; all publications, organizations, Web sites, and other resources exist as described in this book; and all have been verified as of November 2006. The authors and Free Spirit Publishing make no warranty or guarantee concerning the information and materials given out by organizations or content found at Web sites, and we are not responsible for any changes that occur after this book's publication. If you find an error or believe that a resource listed here is not as described, please contact Free Spirit Publishing. Parents, teachers, and other adults: We strongly urge you to monitor children's use of the Internet.

The survey results on page 2 were reported in *Aggravating Circumstances: A Status Report on Rudeness in America*. New York: Public Agenda, 2002.

Design by Marieka Heinlen

10 9 8 7 6 5 4 3 2
Printed in Hong Kong

Free Spirit Publishing Inc.
217 Fifth Avenue North, Suite 200
Minneapolis, MN 55401-1299
(612) 338-2068
help4kids@freespirit.com
www.freespirit.com

Free Spirit Publishing is a member of the Green Press Initiative, and we're committed to printing our books on recycled paper containing a minimum of 30% post-consumer waste (PCW). For every ton of books printed on 30% PCW recycled paper, we save 5.1 trees, 2,100 gallons of water, 114 gallons of oil, 18 pounds of air pollution, 1,230 kilo-watt hours of energy, and .9 cubic yards of landfill space. At Free Spirit it's our goal to nurture not only young people, but nature too!

green press INITIATIVE

Dedication

To Jonah,
who turned out
polite after all.
—PLE

To Olivia and Kristen,
for your wise and entertaining
insights about growing up.
—EHV

Contents

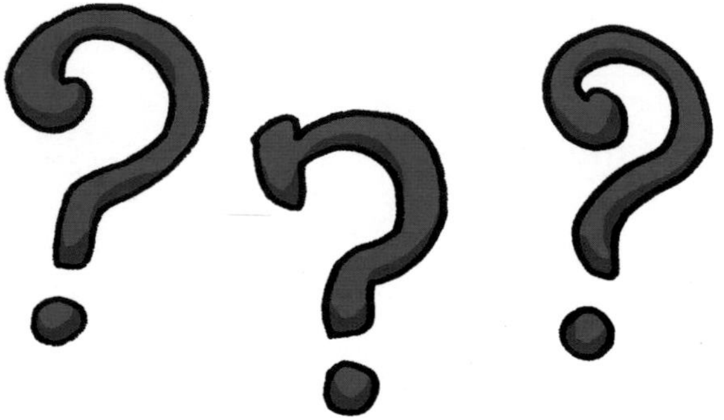

Quick Quiz

Manners are:

1. A. a secret code only snobs know
   B. good behaviors anyone can learn

2. A. silly things you'll hardly ever use
   B. skills you'll use for the rest of your life

3. A. signs that you only care about Y-O-U
   B. signs that you care about other people *and* yourself

4. A. rules invented to make life miserable
   B. rules meant to make life more pleasant

5. A. old-fashioned—no one needs them anymore
   B. as important today as ever, maybe even *more* important

Answers: All Bs for B-have.

1

Manners: Who Cares?

Does it seem like we live in a rude, rude world?

8 out of 10 American adults say a lack of respect and courtesy is a serious problem.

6 out of 10 say things are getting worse.

More than 4 out of 10 admit they sometimes behave pretty badly themselves.

And they're *really* concerned about the rude behavior of children.

What's the big deal about manners, anyway? So what if people sneeze on you, kick your seat during a movie, cut in front of you in line, hog dessert, or spread nasty rumors? Who cares? Well, *you* care. Because it feels bad when people are rude to you—and it feels bad when you're rude to them.

You might not think so at first, but it can sneak up on you later. Like when you remember the look on your friend's face after you dissed him. Or when you think about how you *still* haven't written your thank-you notes for your birthday last year.

When you have manners, you know how to act in all kinds of situations. You don't have to guess or wonder if you're doing something "wrong." That can build your confidence. When you're polite at home, at school, and everywhere else you go, people will notice. They'll see that you're thoughtful, great to know, and fun to be around.

Manners make life easier and nicer for everyone—and that's why manners matter.

 We are not the Manners Police. We're not here to tell you that from now on, you have to be Miss or Mister Perfect. The fact is that wet willies, armpit farts, ding-dong ditch, and other rude noises and tricks are part of being a kid. Don't stop being a kid (at least, not right away). There's a time to goof off and a time to get some, you know—manners. They really do come in handy.

4

Power Words

These words are your manners vocabulary. In a world where many people grab, grunt, shove, and snarl, using these words will set you apart and make you shine.

SAY WHAT?	WHEN?
Please	When you want something
Thank you	When you get it
You're welcome	When someone thanks you
Excuse me*	When you burp, yawn, fart, interrupt a conversation, bump into someone, etc.
Yes, please	When you want something being offered to you
No, thank you	When you don't
I'm sorry	When you mess up

*Excuse Me is an all-purpose courtesy phrase. You can use it in lots of different situations. Like when you're in a hurry and need to get by someone ("Excuse me!"). Or you want to escape a boring conversation ("Excuse me."). Or you're trying to attract someone's attention ("Excuse me . . ."). Or you don't understand what someone just said ("Excuse me?"). Or you want to show how shocked you are by someone else's bad behavior, but in a polite way ("Excuuuse me?"). For extra points, say it in French: *Excusez-moi* (Ek-skyoo-zay-mwa). For fun, try "Ex-squeeze-me."

P.U. Words

These are words and phrases to avoid, unless you want people to think you're a clod.

Shut up
Get Lost
Big deal
So what
You suck
Whatever

Other P.U. words include swear words, often called *four-letter words,* though some have more letters than that. Go to page 80 for more on swears.

In the House

YOO HOO

You're watching a cool show and it's right in the middle of the good part. From another room, your mom calls your name. You ignore her the first time—because *you're right in the middle of the good part.* She calls your name louder. You turn up the volume on the remote. She calls again. In the back of your brain, you have unmannerly thoughts like "Can't she figure out I'm busy?" and "If I pretend not to hear her, maybe she'll leave me alone."

Next thing you know, she's standing in front of the TV, and she doesn't look happy.

"*Mom,* you're blocking the screen."

"Didn't you hear me calling you?"

"I'm watching something!" (You're not exactly lying.)

"Not anymore you're not," she replies, turning off the TV. "I asked you an hour ago to take out the trash, and it's not done. No more TV tonight."

"No fair! Thanks a lot for making me miss the best part of the show!" You stomp to the trashcan and grab the bag—too hard—and accidentally spill a bunch of garbage on the floor.

Your mom watches with her arms crossed, shakes her head, and walks away. Now you're picking up smelly garbage by yourself, and both of you feel bad.

Could a little etiquette have changed things here?
Well, yes.

WhO KNEW? *Etiquette* (EH-tih-ket) is another word
for *manners.* It comes from a French word meaning
ticket. Long ago, when people visited royal palaces in
France, they were given little cards
(tickets) with instructions for how to
behave. That's so they wouldn't do
something stupid and get in trouble
with the king.

Manners Make Life Better

A wise person✳ once described manners as "the happy way of doing things." The key word here is *happy*. That whole scene with the TV and ignoring your mom? Totally could have been avoided. All you had to do was take out the trash when she asked.

✳No, it wasn't Yoda. It was Marjabelle Young Stewart, an expert on etiquette.

What if you forgot and sat down in front of the TV? The first time your mom called your name, you could have hit the mute button and answered, "Yes, Mom?" When she reminded you to take out the trash, you could have said, "Wow, I'm sorry, I totally forgot!" Then you could have said, "I'll do it now." Or maybe, "I'm watching a show and it's right in the middle of the good part—can I please take out the trash when it's over?" Because you asked so nicely, she could have said yes.

And now a few words about family. They're the people you wake up with, share a bathroom with, and come home to. They know your history, your favorite foods, your worst moods, and what you'd ask for if a genie popped out of a bottle and gave you three wishes. How many people can you say *that* about? So they're more than just Dad, Mom, Grandma, Sis, Bro, or Uncle Bob—they're the people who take care of you and care about you. You may not have chosen them, but they're *yours*, and they love you.

And that's why (big surprise coming up . . . wait for it . . . **wait . . .**)

Your family
deserves
Your very

BEST

Manners.

Often, we use our very *worst* manners around our families. We ignore them, complain to them, sulk and whine around them, or burp at top volume in their presence. Some of us don't think twice about grabbing the last serving of mashed potatoes before anyone else does or sneaking peaks at other family members' email. That's just *rude*.

Oh, Behave!
(Tips for Better Family Manners)

1. Start out right. When you get up, greet your family with a smile and say "Good morning." You won't believe what a difference this can make. Before going to bed, give hugs or kisses and say "Goodnight."

2. Tune in. You probably like it when people pay attention to you, laugh at your stories and jokes, and care that you exist. Do you show this same courtesy to your family? Don't ignore your dad or roll your eyes every time your sister opens her mouth.

3. Watch what you say. When your parents try to talk to you, do you grunt and mumble? Or say a lot of "Yo," "I dunno," or "Whatever"? Try speaking clearly and using full sentences. You get bonus points for telling them about what you did in school all day and asking how *they're* doing.

4. Respect your home. Please stop wiping your greasy chip-covered fingers on the couch cushions and leaving dirty footprints everywhere you go. Cleaning up after yourself is big—it's HUGE. Your family will love it when you're neat and helpful.

5. Respect people's stuff. If you want to borrow something, ask first. Treat your family's belongings with care. Don't raid your dad's wallet or dig through your mom's purse. Never listen in on private phone calls or read anyone's journal or mail, no matter how curious you are.

6. Knock first.
A closed door means something, so get in the habit of knocking before entering. Then wait for a "Come in." Even if the door to someone's room is open, it's polite to rap on it to give the person some warning that you're standing there. Never barge into a bedroom or bathroom when the door is closed.

Oops

7. Keep it down. Do you blast your music, the TV, the computer, or your video games? Or yell from room to room instead of finding the person you need? When you go up and down stairs, does it sound like **a herd of elephants?** If you turn down the volume, people won't have to shush you so much.

8. Be responsible. You're not in kindergarten anymore, so you can get up when your alarm goes off, make your own snacks, and even do your chores without being asked. This is a guaranteed way to get noticed, in a good way, at home.

9. Say "Please" and "Thank you." For other important manners words, see page 4.

10. Talk to your family about what's okay and what's not. Maybe your family has relaxed rules about burping or telling gross stories at the table. And maybe there's a different set of expectations for when you have company. Make sure you know what kind of behavior is okay and when. If your family doesn't seem to know much about manners, you might share some of the ideas in this book with them.

P.S. Change can start with you. Look for adults who have good manners and learn from them. Be a manners role model for your siblings. Try the ten tips above—make them a habit at home—and see if your family life improves.

Body Manners

Hey, you—the one with your finger up your nose. You *really* need to read this part. It's about the human body and some of the stuff that comes out of it. You know, the stuff you can see (boogers and spit and phlegm), the stuff you can hear (burps and hiccups and yawns), and the stuff you can smell (farts).

Nose Picking

You've been hearing it since you were two: It's not polite to pick your nose around other people. Pickin' and lickin' is too gross for words—and booger inspection is off-limits. Never chase your sister with your boogers. If you must pick, do it in private (find a bathroom). Use a tissue and wash your hands afterward. Toss the tissue in the trash.

Nose Blowing

Use a tissue when you blow your nose. Whenever possible, wash your hands afterward. A tissue can only hold so much, and usually you're left with *something* on your hands. Toss zee tissue in zee trash.

Clue4U Keep a small container of instant hand-cleaning liquid in your pocket, backpack, or desk for times when you can't get to a sink to wash up. Or stash pre-packaged hand wipes in handy places.

Sneezing and Coughing

You can't help it if you have to sneeze—but you can make sure you don't spray everyone around you when you do. If you feel a sneeze coming on, grab a tissue or cover your nose and mouth with the crook of your arm.

Who Knew? *Gesundheit* (geh-ZOONT-hyte) is a German word that means *health*. Germans (and many Americans) say it when someone sneezes. In Italy, people say *felicita* (fe-LEE-see-ta), which means *happiness*. In Japan, when people sneeze, no one says anything special.

The same goes for coughs: Make every effort to cover them up, but *not with your hand*. Why? Because your hand will be crawling with germs, and the next time you high-five someone, that person's hand will be crawling with them, too. Instead, turn your head away and cough into the crook of your arm or into your shoulder.

BLECCCHHH

Remember, when the phlegm flies, other people get sprayed with *your* germs. Covering up coughs and sneezes—the right way—shows good manners and prevents the spread of illness.

Just like with nose blowing, wash your hands after you cough or sneeze, or wipe up with some instant hand cleaner.

Gesundheit

Fancy-Pants Manners

If you hear *Ah, ah, ah . . .* it means a *CHOO!* isn't far behind. Grab a tissue and hand it to the sneezer. It's the polite way to avoid getting sprayed.

Spitting

If you get caught spitting in Singapore, you'll have to pay a fine. Spitting in public isn't a crime in the United States, but it's sure to draw some dirty looks. So don't:

- Spit unwanted food onto your plate *

- Drool on your friends

- Hawk a loogie (clear your throat *arghh braghh urghhhh* and spit out the results)

- Use a water fountain as your personal spit catcher

*What *should* you do with it? See page 43.

Yawning

No matter how tired or bored you are, a big, noisy yawn with your mouth wide open is rude. No one wants to see the inside of your mouth or that floppy little thing that hangs down from the back of your throat.* Yawning in your teacher's face during class is not only rude, it's risky.

*It's called your *uvula*, if you care.

When you can't stop a yawn, place your hand over your mouth—as you breathe in *and* as you breathe out. Follow up with "Excuse me!" if you yawn while someone is talking to you.

Chew on This!
(Gummy Manners)

Gum is gooey. That's part of its appeal. But gooey is gross when someone else's gum ends up on *you* because you touched it, stepped in it, or sat on it.

Many schools ban gum chewing. Teachers and principals don't want to see you having fun with your gum by stretching, snapping, twisting, popping, and offering your ABC (Already Been Chewed) wad to the person sitting next to you. They don't want to spot a huge pink bubble hiding your face, hear that horrid *popping* sound, and have to pick the gum-gunk out of your hair.

When you do chew, the whole world doesn't have to know. Try to minimize the sound effects. Keep your lips closed. Kindly offer a piece to your friends.

Avoid sticking old gum behind your ear, on your plate, under your chair, in the car's cup-holder, or on the ground. Wrap it in a tissue or a piece of paper first, then drop it in the trash.

Burps

All you pros out there can probably burp loud enough for the kids in the next class to hear you . . . or burp the ABCs on command. You can bring up a silent-but-deadly one that you blow down the table toward your brother as he innocently eats his dinner. Is it funny? Kinda.✳ Is it rude? Mostly.

✳Oh, all right. Burping is more than kinda funny. It's absolutely HILARIOUS—but *at the right times.* Go ahead and have burping contests with your friends. Rate your mega-belches on a scale from one to ten. Just don't do it around grown-ups or people you want to impress (like that cute guy or girl you're suddenly interested in).

It's good manners to burp as softly as possible with your hand placed over your mouth, and then say "Excuse me" afterward. If a friend burps, don't go "That was *excellent!*" and beg for more. Post-burp analysis isn't required. Pretend you didn't notice and move on.

Hiccups

Hiccups sneak up on you when you least expect them. If you get them, don't make them louder on purpose or fake a few in-between *hics* to start the whole class laughing. Say "Excuse me," then wait them out. Hiccups pass.

And so does . . .

Gas

Here's some simple Manners Math:

Farts +

Etiquette

= Fartiquette

The rules of fartiquette are simple. Try to keep the laughter, finger pointing, and comments to a minimum. Hold back your urge to go, "*P.U.!* Who cut the cheese?" Refrain from sniffing deeply and remarking about the quality of the smell.

If you're the one who dealt it, you don't have to admit it. Just act like it never happened. If you're with family members or close friends and they know it was you, say a quick "Sorry!" and go back to whatever it was you were doing before you let one rip. That's passing gas with class.

What if you're at school and you feel a butt blast coming on?

According to an anonymous fourth-grade expert: "Just let it out really slowly a little at a time so no one hears." Or excuse yourself and head to the bathroom, where you can fart to your heart's content.

Who Knew?

Passing gas is totally normal. Everyone does it. Most people do it about 14 times a day, producing about 1 to 4 pints of natural gas. The good news is, most farts don't smell. When they do, it's usually because of bacteria in the large intestine. Those bacteria release small amounts of gases that contain sulfur—the same stuff that makes rotten eggs so stinky.

Clue 4 U Have you heard of the "magical fruit"? ("The more you eat, the more you toot.") If you're going to be in a confined space with other people for a period of time—a classroom, a car trip, or a plane ride—think ahead. Don't load up on beans, broccoli, bananas, or anything else that turns you into a gas bag.

Clean Up Your Act
(Ways to Have a Tidy Body)

1. Wash your face. Don't leave home with a milk mustache. Make it a habit to wash your face in the morning (and before bed, too). Save face by using a napkin when you eat.

2. Wash your bod. Between school, sports, and playing, you get dirty. So keep your body clean by taking baths or showers more often. Afterward, put on clean clothes—not ones you fished out of the hamper.

3. Try some hair care. You'll feel and look better when you take care of your hair. You don't have to blow a month's allowance on products—just use a basic shampoo, conditioner, and gel or mousse (if needed). Get regular haircuts and run a brush or comb through your hair once in a while.

4. Sniff those pits. You're at an age when you might start noticing some funky smells coming from your armpits. You (and everyone around you) will breathe easier if you use deodorant or antiperspirant.

5. Brush and floss. To keep your mouth clean and fresh, brush your teeth at least twice a day (after breakfast and before bed). Whenever possible, brush after eating sugary snacks or drinking soda. Ask your mom or dad, or the dentist, how to floss correctly, then floss each night. To beat bad breath, use mints, mouthwash, or breath spray.

6. Have neat feet. Feet can get sweaty, so wash them often. Make sure to wear clean socks and air out your shoes after school and sports. And no matter how clean you think your bare feet are, don't put them on the coffee table or rest them on other people.

7. Notice your nails. See if they're dirty, ragged, or bitten down. Keep them clean, trim them as needed, and try not to bite them.

8. Check your habits. Do you suck on your shirt-sleeves or hair, or pick at your zits or scabs? Does your finger often find its way into your nose or ears? Don't look now, but people are probably watching when you do these things—and it's not a pretty sight.

9. Stand up straight. Are you a slumper? A sloucher? Well, stand up straighter. You'll look taller, stronger, and more confident.

10. Smile. You've got a great smile—why not share it? You'll automatically seem more polite when you show those pearly whites.

 What about booty-scratching and wedgie-picking? Both should be done when no one's looking. If needed, create a distraction like, "Hey, what's that over there?" while pointing in the opposite direction. When everyone turns their heads, pick and scratch quickly.

Potty Manners

Have you learned the rules of polite pottying?

Do say "Excuse me, I'll be right back" if you're around other people. If you're in school, raise your hand and ask your teacher if you can be excused for a restroom break. If you're at a friend's home, ask "May I please use your bathroom?"

Don't make a Public Service Announcement (PSA) like "Boy oh boy, I *really* have to pee!" while holding your hands over your privates.

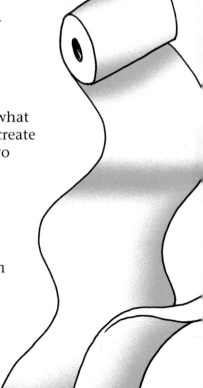

Do use toilet paper—but only what you need. Huge clumps could create a clog. If you must use a lot, two flushes are better than one.

Don't use up all of the toilet paper and forget to change the roll. It's polite to consider the next person's needs. If you're in a restaurant or another public place, tell a worker that the bathroom is out of TP.

Do use this time to admire your surroundings. Gaze out the window, check out the décor, or pick up a magazine if there's one handy.

Don't use this time to decorate the stall walls. If you're tempted to respond to graffiti with clever lines of your own, resist.

Do tuck in your shirt, zip your fly, and make yourself presentable afterward. If you're wearing a skirt, check to make sure it isn't caught up in your waistband, or people will see London, France, and your underpants.

Don't walk out the door with toilet paper trailing off your shoe.

Do respect other's people's privacy.

Don't barge in on your sister, bang on the door the whole time your brother is in the can, or peek under the stall doors at school.

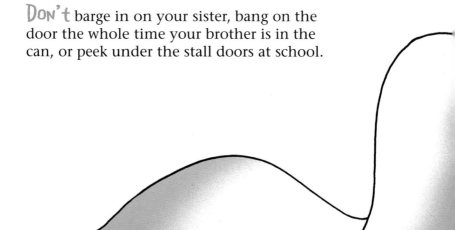

Boys: Please put the seat down when you're done. No unsuspecting female likes to fall into the toilet in the middle of the night because *someone* forgot to put the seat down.

Girls: Hey, drips happen. Be a sweetie and wipe the seatie.

Do flush.

Don't forget to flush.

Do wash your hands afterward.

Don't wipe your hands on your pants and consider the job done.

Handy Hints
(The Right Way to Wash Up)

1. Use warm water and plenty of soap.

2. Scrub for at least 30 seconds. (That's enough time to hum the *Jeopardy* theme song in your head. You know the one: *Dum, dum, dum, dum, dee, dee, dee . . .*)

3. Rinse well and dry your hands with a clean towel or paper towel.

4. Avoid touching the (germy) door handle with your clean hands. Grip it with a paper towel or your shirtsleeve instead.

Eating

The Goops they lick their fingers,
And the Goops they lick their knives;
They spill their broth on the
tablecloth—
Oh, they lead disgusting lives!
The Goops they talk while eating,
And loud and fast they chew;
And that is why I'm glad that I
Am not a Goop—are you?

A man named Gelett Burgess wrote this poem more than 100 years ago. Too bad more people haven't read it, because the world is full of Goops. Look around the school cafeteria . . . your favorite fast-food restaurant . . . maybe even the dinner table at home. See any Goops?

Lucky for you, table manners aren't hard to learn. And you get to practice them three times a day.

The Top 10 Table Manners Kids Need to Know

According to parents, these are the table manners that matter most.

1. Come to the table when you're called. Arrive at the table neat and clean—hands and face washed, hair brushed, hat off.*

   *At the table, a hood counts as a hat.

2. Put your napkin in your lap as soon as you sit down. Sit up straight and keep your elbows off the table.

3. Wait to start eating until everyone at the table has been served.

4. Take small bites and chew with your mouth closed. Eat slowly and quietly (no gobbling). Don't smack your lips, gulp your drink, swish, slosh, burp on purpose, or blow bubbles. Swallow before you speak.

5. Take part in the conversation at the table. Don't chat on the phone, text your friends, listen to headphones, or read.*

   *Some families relax these rules at breakfast, when it's okay to read the newspaper or the cereal box.

6. If you need to leave the table during the meal, say "Please excuse me for a moment."

7. If something gets stuck in your teeth, excuse yourself and head for the bathroom.

8. If you can't reach something you want, ask some-one to please pass it to you.

9. Say "Thank you" at the end of the meal. Then ask, "May I be excused?"

10. Help clear the table without waiting to be asked.

 Put simply, eat like a person, not a pig. **Oink.**

Hungry for More?

Want to know a few more tasty table manners? Try these.

- Offer serving plates to other people at the table before you serve yourself.

- Pass serving dishes to the right.

- Pass the salt and pepper together, even if someone just asks for the salt.

- When you eat salad, cut it into bite-sized pieces. Never smoosh a giant lettuce leaf into your mouth.

- When you eat soup, move your spoon from the front or middle to the back of the bowl.✶ (Then you won't slosh soup on your shirt or into your lap.) Sip, don't slurp.

✶It helps to remember this rhyme: *Just like ships go out to sea/ I spoon my soup away from me.*

- Sample food before salting it. If you salt before sampling, you could insult the cook.

- Instead of washing chewed food down with your drink, swallow, *then* sip.

How to Eat a Roll

Just butter and bite, right? Not quite.

1. Put a dab of butter on your plate (or your bread plate, if you have one).

2. Break off a piece of the roll.

3. Butter only that piece.

4. Eat.

5. Repeat.

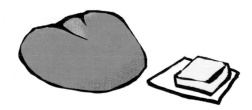

Dining Out

If you use good table manners at home (see pages 34–36), dining out will be easy. You won't have to become a completely different person or act in whole new ways. You may even need to dress up, which can be kind of fun. And instead of eating what everyone else eats, you'll get to pick something you want off the menu.

- At the restaurant, don't run to reach the table first and take the best seat. Calmly walk to your table, sit down, put your napkin on your lap, and begin to read your menu.

- If you don't see a single thing you like on the menu, look again. Try to be flexible. Order something simple, like buttered noodles.

- If your fork, knife, or spoon falls on the floor, leave it. Politely ask the server for a new one.

- If you spill, drip, drop, or slosh, don't panic. Accidents happen, and servers know what to do.

- In fast-food restaurants, cafeterias, and some delis, you carry your own food to the table, and you're expected to pick up after yourself. Toss your trash and recycling, put dirty dishes where they belong, and stack your tray.

- Thank whoever paid for the meal, even if it's Mom or Dad.

Clue 4 U Is it okay to eat chicken drumsticks with your fingers? What on earth do you do with shish kebob or corn on the cob? When in doubt, watch what other people do. Not the toddler in the high chair, but the grown-ups around you. Ditto for a restaurant, friend's house, or special event dinner, like a wedding or graduation.

The Place-Setting Puzzle

It's a special occasion, and you've been invited to a fancy restaurant. You get dressed up, follow the grown-ups to the table, take your seat, put your napkin on your lap, and—eek! What are you supposed to do with all those plates, glasses, and utensils?

Don't freak. Solving the place-setting puzzle is simple if you remember three rules:

1. Your glass is the one on the RIGHT. Your bread plate is the one on the LEFT.

2. Use utensils from the outside-in. Start with the spoon on your far RIGHT. Start with the fork on your far LEFT.

Clue 4 U A salad fork is smaller than a dinner fork. A soup spoon is bigger than a teaspoon.

3. When in doubt, *watch what other people do.* Or ask an adult for advice. Grown-ups don't mind when a polite young person says, "Excuse me, but could you tell me what this funny-looking fork is for?"

Smooth Moves in Sticky Situations

THE PROBLEM

WHAT TO DO

Someone serves you noodles with peanut sauce. You're allergic to peanuts.

Say, "This looks delicious, but unfortunately, I'm allergic to peanuts."

Someone serves you something you've never eaten before, but you think it might be yucky.

Try at least one bite if you can, then eat it if you like it. If you don't like it, cut it into smaller pieces and push them around on your plate. This will look as if you're eating it (sort of).

Someone asks you if you'd like something you already know is yucky.

Say, "No, thank you. I don't care for any."

THE PROBLEM

You eat a bite of something and it really *is* yucky.

You find a creepy-crawly bug, a hair, or something else disgusting in your salad.

WHAT TO DO

Quietly remove it from your mouth with your finger and thumb, then set it on one side of your plate.✻

Try not to jump up and scream your head off. Say, "May I please have another salad?"

✻This is also how to handle gristle, olive pits, fish bones, and other things you can't or shouldn't chew.

The School Cafeteria

Sometimes eating in the school cafeteria seems like survival of the fittest. The food flies. Kids push. Milk spills. Chairs tip. And everywhere you look, you see examples of gross behavior.

You can't change other people's manners, but you can mind your own. Just the basics will set you apart from the crowd: Keep your elbows off the table, chew with your mouth closed, and don't talk with food in your mouth. When you're done eating, pick up after yourself.

What about the fun stuff? Sorry, but the school cafeteria isn't the place for rude food. Which means no:

Noodle-slurping

Pea-flicking

Soda-spraying

Milk-gargling

"See food"

Straws in your nose

Saying "Ewww!

Your lunch stinks!"

Wiping fingers on friends

Cafeteria workers are people, too. Saying "Hi! How's it going?" can make their day. If there's someone you see a lot, learn his or her name. Then you can say "Hey, Mrs. D! What's up?" Bet this gets you the biggest burger or best brownie.

Meeting & Greeting

It's fun to meet new people. And it's not hard or scary once you know the Ancient Ritual, the Magic Words, and the Secret Handshake.

This is the Ancient Ritual:

1. Stand up if you're sitting down.

2. Smile.

3. Look the other person in the eye.

4. Move toward him or her.

If you're shy, you might not like looking people in the eye. Try this trick: Ask yourself, "I wonder what color eyes the person has?" Then take a look and find out.

Clue4U

These are the Magic Words:

Hello. My name is

_____.

(your name)

I'm glad to meet you.

Fancy-Pants Manners

Instead of "Hello," say, "How do you do?" Or "How dooo you dooooooo?"

If you want, you can also say a little something about yourself. Not a braggy something, but a simple fact or two. If you can, make a connection between yourself and someone else the person knows.

I go to Jefferson School, and I'm in the fifth grade.

I'm Sasha's brother.

This is the Secret Handshake:

1. Hold out your RIGHT hand (even if you're a lefty) with your thumb up and palm flat.

2. Grasp the other person's hand. Don't go limp or squeeze too hard.

3. Pump your hand up and down once or twice.

4. Let go.

Introductions

Sometimes people will count on you to help them meet each other. This happens when you host a party and not everyone knows everyone else, or two friends of yours meet for the first time, or you invite a new friend over. When you introduce people to each other, they stop being strangers, and it's all because of you.

Introductions are easy. Say this:

> Amber, this is Tiffany.
> Tiffany, this is Amber.

Or this:

> Amber, I'd like to introduce
> you to my friend Tiffany.
> Tiffany, meet Amber.

Be sure to say each person's name twice. And be sure to say each person's name *clearly*. Not:

> Mmmff, this is Hrrrrm.
> Hrrrrm, this is Mmmff.

If you want, you can add a small detail about each person. This gives them something to talk about right away.

> Amber, this is Tiffany.
> Tiffany has a Siamese
> cat named Mr. Boo. Amber
> is in my scout troop.

Make sure the detail is positive and not too personal. Amber doesn't need to know that Tiffany just got over a bad case of head lice. Tiffany doesn't need to know that Amber is scared of the dark.

You probably have permission to call some adults by their first names, but it's still good manners to use their titles when making introductions:

- Mr. for a man

- Mrs. for a married woman

- Ms. for a woman (married or not)

- Miss for a girl or unmarried woman

 If you don't know whether to call a woman Miss, Ms., or Mrs., ask her what she wants to be called.

Fancy-Pants Manners When you introduce an older person to a younger person, say the older person's name first ("Mrs. Delgado, this is Tiffany. Tiffany, this is Mrs. Delgado"). If one person is a VIP (Very Important Person), like the school principal, the President of the United States, or an Imperial Poobah, say his or her title and name first ("Imperial Poobah Peterson, this is D.J. D.J., this is Imperial Poobah Peterson").

Smooth Moves in Sticky Situations

THE PROBLEM	WHAT TO DO
When you're introduced to someone new, you usually forget the person's name right away.	Repeat the person's name when you're introduced, then say it two or three more times right away. Like this: "Hi, Mimi, I'm glad to meet you. Where do you go to school, Mimi? . . . You're a dancer? Cool, Mimi. . . . It was fun meeting you, Mimi. Bye, Mimi!" She may think you're kind of nutty, but you won't forget her name.
You're introducing two people when you totally blank on one of their names.	Try introducing the person you do know ("This is Amber"). If you're lucky, the other person will jump in and say his or her name ("Hi, Amber, I'm D.J.").

THE PROBLEM

You're introducing two people when you totally blank on *both* of their names.

WHAT TO DO

Come clean. You might say, "Oh my gosh, I'm such a dope! I'm sorry, but I've forgotten both of your names. Please tell me again."

You're visiting a friend's house for the first time, and your friend forgets to introduce you to his mom.

Don't just ignore her. She's not a piece of furniture. Ask your friend to introduce you. Or go up to her and say, "Hi, I'm (your name). Thank you for letting D.J. invite me over. What should I call you?" Your friend's mom will be very impressed.

Even with people you see every day, it's good to give a friendly greeting. Start with your family in the morning. Say hi to your friends throughout the day. Say hello to your teachers. Never walk into a friend's home without greeting his or her parents. When you leave, say "Thank you" and "Goodbye."

Hosting & Guesting

When you're a host, follow Rule #1: *Guests go first.*

When you're a guest, follow Rule #2: *Act like you don't know Rule #1.*

Confusing? Not if you remember that manners are about making *others* feel good.

Hosting

Even if your invitation is super-casual ("Hey D.J., want to come over after school and play video games?"), it's your job as host to make your guest feel welcome and comfortable.

Start by showing him where to put his stuff (coat, backpack, and shoes if your home is a shoes-off zone). Introduce him to your parent(s). This is the time to say what to call them.

Mom, this is my friend D.J.
D.J., this is my mom, Brenda.

Dad, this is my friend D.J.
D.J., this is my stepdad, Mr. Newman.

Do other adults live with you? Introduce them, too.

> Grandma, this is my friend D.J.
> D.J., this is my grandma,
> Mrs. Waldenstein.

Nice work! Next, offer your friend something to eat and drink.

> Want a sandwich?

Yum. Thanks!

Only now do you head for the TV and video games. Where (because you're a well-mannered host) you let your friend pick the game, take the first turn—*and use your stuff without acting like it pains you to do so.*

No wonder everyone loves coming to your house.

Party Smarts

you're having
a par-tay . . .
gonna have a
good time . . . .

Not unless you invite people. You can do this in many different ways: face-to-face, over the phone, by text message or instant message, by email, or by snail mail. Do it one or two weeks ahead of time.

In your invitation, let people know:

1. Who's hosting the party (y-O-u)

2. When the party will happen (day, date, starting time, ending time)

3. Where the party will happen (your address or another location)

4. What kind of party it is (birthday, sleepover, barbecue)

5. Anything else your guests need to know—if the party has a theme, if they need to bring anything, if they should wear special clothes, if food and drinks will be served

This is a lot to cover face-to-face or over the phone. What if you need to include a map or directions? You can send written information and maps by email, but what about spam filters that block some emails? What about friends who don't have computers?

Written invitations are still the best. You can buy preprinted invitations at stores or **deSiGN yOur OwN.** You can hand them out in person or send them through the mail. If you hand them out in person, *be sure not to do it in front of people you're not inviting.* Ouch, that hurts.

TO: D.J.
FROM: Bart
IT'S PARTY TIME!
WHAT: Make-your-Own-Pizza
WHEN: Saturday, January 22,
    5-8 P.M.
WHERE: My place (see the map)
WHY: Because it's my birthday
    and pizza rocks!

Bring or wear clothes you don't care about.
Plus we'll eat snacks, play games, and have prizes!
RSVP: 612-555-7383 by Thursday, January 20

R-S-V-Please

RSVP is French for *Répondez, s'il vous plaît* (Ray-pon-day, see-voo-play). The exact translation is *Respond, if you please,* but what it really means is *Tell me if you're coming or not.*

It's rude not to RSVP, but a lot of people don't seem to know that.✶ You can't change other people's bad manners. If some of the kids on your guest list don't RSVP, you'll have to call them and ask if they'll be there. Otherwise, you won't know how much pizza dough to have on hand, or how many prizes.

✶But now *you* do. So whenever you get an invitation, be sure to RSVP. How soon? No later than three days after the invitation arrives. This is called the *three-day rule.* Duh.

Party Manners

You're the birthday person, and the party is in your honor. Does that mean you don't have to act like a host? Nope. It's still up to you to make sure people have a good time.

- Plan activities ahead of time—dancing, games, sports, swimming, and other things you think your friends would like to do.

- Greet your guests as they arrive.

- Introduce people to each other.

- Every once in a while, check the snacks and drinks to make sure they haven't run out.

- Spend time with *all* of your guests, not just your best friends.

- When it's time for birthday cake, make a wish, blow out the candles—and serve your guests first.

Guesting

You come home from school and check your mail. A letter from Grandpa . . . a postcard from your pen pal in Peru . . . and an invitation to Bart's bash!

The first thing you do is get permission to go. The next thing you do is RSVP: You call Bart and tell him. On Saturday, your mom takes you to the mall so you can shop for a birthday present. You buy a giant chef's hat that says PIZZA PRO because you know Bart will get a laugh out of wearing it.

On the day of the party, you remember to put on an old, beat-up T-shirt. You arrive on time, say hi to Bart's parents, and spend a few minutes talking with them. Then you head for the kitchen, have a blast making pizza, eat a lot, laugh a lot, and talk to everyone there. Of course, Bart thinks your present is hilarious.

At the end of the party, when your mom is a few minutes late picking you up, you offer to help clean up. On your way out, you tell Bart and his parents, "Thanks for inviting me! I had a great time!"

No wonder people love having you over.

The Dreamy Sleepover

A sleepover (or longer stay—like a weekend or a week) is different from a same-day party. You're not just going for a short visit. You're living in someone else's home for a period of time.

You're eating there, changing clothes there, sleeping there (sort of), and brushing your teeth there. And even though your hosts may say to "make yourself at home," it's not really your home. So you can't do some of the things you might do around your house, like put your feet on the coffee table or your toothbrush in the medicine cabinet.

Clue4U When you arrive for a sleepover or any kind of party, be sure to say hi to your friend's parents. If you don't see them, ask where they are. If it turns out they're not around, ask if you can use the telephone. Then call your parents and tell them to come and get you, because you don't go to parties in homes where the adults are away.

Here's everything you need to know to be a great guest.

★ When you arrive, don't just dump your stuff anywhere. Ask where to put your coat, shoes, and overnight bag.

★ Bring your own bathroom things—toothbrush, toothpaste, hairbrush—so you don't have to borrow your friend's.

★ Be a good sport. Go along with whatever games and activities your hosts have planned.

★ Try to be nice to everyone, including your friend's little sister. And even if you're not having fun, try to act like you are.

★ Follow the house rules. Watch to see what your friend does.

★ If you want to use the phone or TV, ask.

★ If you're hungry, don't just go to the fridge and help yourself. Ask if you can please have something to eat.

★ Respect people's privacy. Don't snoop in their stuff.

★ Use good bathroom manners (see pages 29–32) and good table manners (see pages 34–36).

★ At meal times, if someone says a blessing, join in or sit quietly.

★ Clean up after yourself. Help your friend with chores.

★ Let your hosts know if you need a nightlight. Ask if you can call home to say goodnight.

★ Be quiet late at night. If you tell ghost stories, whisper.

★ When you leave, say "Thanks for inviting me. I had a good time." You may want to write a thank-you note. See pages 71–73.

Fancy-Pants Manners

When you arrive for an overnight or longer stay, it's thoughtful to bring along a gift for your friend's mom or dad—like some homemade cookies or a picture you've drawn. This will make your host think you're the most polite and thoughtful kid in the world.

Smooth Moves in Sticky Situations

THE PROBLEM

WHAT TO DO

You're having a party and you can only invite four friends. Another friend who isn't invited finds out about it. She's too polite to say so, but you can tell her feelings are hurt.

Tell your friend that your parents are only letting you invite a few people. Say it's not your choice, and you'll do something special with her soon. Then do.

You totally forgot to RSVP to an invitation. It's the day of the party, and you want to go.

Don't just show up. Call your friend. Apologize for forgetting to RSVP. Ask if it's okay if you come to the party anyway. If your friend says no for whatever reason, say that you understand and wish him a good time.

Ten people RSVP to your party, promising to come. Only three show up.

Try not to act too disappointed. Have a good time with the friends who are there. Afterward, find new friends.

THE PROBLEM

WHAT TO DO

You promise to go to a friend's sleepover. Then another friend invites you to a sleepover on the same day.

Tough toenails. You already said yes to the first friend, and that's where you should go. The *only* exception is if something super-special, once-in-a-lifetime comes along. Be honest and your friend will probably understand.

You use the bathroom at a friend's house and clog up the toilet.

Don't pretend it didn't happen. Someone will find out sooner or later. Even though it's embarrassing, tell your friend. Better yet, tell your friend's mom or dad. You can just say, "Excuse me, but there's a problem with the toilet."

You're visiting a friend's house and you break or damage something. No one saw you do it.

Don't blame the dog (especially if the family doesn't have a dog). Admit what happened and say you're sorry. If possible, offer to replace it, fix it, or have it cleaned. Chances are, your hosts won't accept, but they will be glad you offered.

Gifting & Getting

Which is more fun—getting a present you really like, or picking out the perfect present for a friend? An old saying goes "It's better to give than receive," but receiving is terrific, too. Here's the right, polite way to do both.

Gifting

Some occasions require gifts. Others don't. These are the ones that usually do:

- Birthdays

- Weddings

- Bridal showers

- Baby showers

- Some religious holidays

You don't have to bring a gift to a just-because party, a sleepover, or a picnic at a friend's house. You probably won't have to spend your own money on wedding or shower gifts. For religious holidays, you'll mainly exchange gifts with family members. So the gifts you mostly need to think about are birthday gifts for friends.

Try to choose something you think the other person will like, even if you don't understand it at all. So your best friend loves polka music. You think it's weird, but you look all over for a CD of polka music anyway. That's being a true friend.

Handmade gifts are just as good as store-bought gifts, sometimes even better. Can you do a fun cartoon of you and your friend? What about making a CD of songs you think your friend will like? Did you ever think of a "gift certificate" for two hours of helping-out-with-chores time?

If you truly don't have a clue about what someone might like, a gift card to a popular store is a good choice.

Wrap your gift neatly. (Take off the price tag first.) Tape a card on top with your name and the name of the person you're giving it to. If you just slide the card under the ribbon, it could fall off, especially at a party where there are lots of gifts.

When you hand your gift to your friend, don't beg your friend to please, please, please open it first. Simply say "I hope you like it." Then let it go—for real. Don't bug your friend about it forever. Don't ask, "Are you listening to the CD I gave you?" "How come you aren't wearing the T-shirt I bought you?" "Where's that cute little horse statue I gave you? I didn't notice it in your room. Did you break it or something? Where is it? Can I see it?"

Clue 4 U How much should you spend on a gift you buy? Ask your dad or mom. What if you can't afford much? Spend less. Some people have more money than others, and gift giving is not a contest.

What if the invitation says "No gifts, please"? Then don't bring any. Your host wants your presence, not your presents.

Getting

When someone gives you a gift, say:

- "Thank you!" if you love it

- "Thank you!" if you like it

- "Thank you!" if you kind of like it

- "Thank you!" if you don't like it at all, and

- "Thank you!" if you totally hate it.

Never say "What *is* this?" or "Wow! This has to be the worst gift ever!" Even if it's true, that would be rude and the gift-giver's feelings would be hurt. You can also say:

- "You are so thoughtful!"

- "How nice of you!"

- "This is so sweet of you!"

- "I really appreciate it that you thought of me."

What to Do with a Gift You Don't Like, Don't Want, or Don't Need (It Happens)

- If it's something useful but it's not your thing, donate it.

- If you know where your friend bought it, you might return it or exchange it for something you like better.

- Another option is to give it to someone else. This is called *re-gifting,* and it can be tricky. You have to make sure not to hurt the giver's feelings. (How would *you* feel if you found out that someone re-gifted a present from you?) Before you re-gift, think it through. Talk with your mom and dad and get their advice.

Or you can always hide the gift away until just before your friend comes over, then hurry and bring it out. The trouble with this is it's hard to remember. Sooner or later, you'll tell your friend to get something out of your closet, and before you know it, your friend will be asking, "Hey, look, here's that little horse statue I gave you! What's it doing in your closet?" Oops.

Thank-You Notes

Some kids would rather **wrestle live alligators** than write thank-you notes. Some kids simply refuse to write thank-you notes, even when their parents yell, "You are not getting the twenty dollars Aunt Beth sent you until you write her a thank-you note!" Since writing a thank-you note takes about two seconds,* this is silly.

*Okay, a little longer than two seconds, but not *that* much longer.

Here's everything you need to know and all you need to do.

1. Get a nice, clean piece of paper. If you want, you can decorate it with stickers and drawings. (The more you decorate, the less you'll have to write because there won't be room.) You can even use a picture postcard. Write your thank-you note *by hand*.

2. Greet the person who gave you the gift.

Dear Aunt Beth,

3. Thank the person for the gift.

Thank you for the $20 you sent me for my birthday.

4. Say something about how you plan to use the gift.

I've been saving up for new skates, and this will really help.

5. Write one sentence that shows interest in the person who gave you the gift.

I hope you and your parakeet are very happy.

Optional: Write one sentence about your family.

We are all looking forward to our vacation in Yellowstone Park this summer.

6. Say thanks again, and sign your name.

Thanks again! Love, Scooter

Handwritten thank-you notes are best, but a thank-you email is better than no note at all.

When to Write a Thank-You Note

- When someone sends you a gift and isn't there to watch you open it.

- When a special grown-up sends you a gift. This might be a grandparent, a godparent, or a favorite aunt or uncle.

- When anyone over 60 years old sends you a gift. Older people can get very upset when kids don't send thank-you notes. Think about their poor old feelings and their poor old hearts.

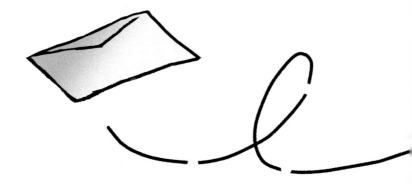

- Three days after you open the gift.＊ What if you forget? Then do it as soon as you remember. It's almost never too late to write a thank-you note. If you wait a really long time, start with an apology.

  ＊Remember the *three-day rule*? (See page 58.) Here it is again.

- When you have been a guest at someone else's home for more than a night. You don't have to send a thank-you note for a sleepover.

- When someone has treated you to something special, like dinner at a fancy restaurant.

- Whenever you wonder "Should I write a thank-you note or not?" It's always safer to write one.

Word-y Manners

Do you ever feel like you don't know what to say? Or like you're always saying the wrong thing? Do you have trouble starting conversations or keeping them going? Follow these steps to build your talking skills.

5 Steps to Good Conversation

1. Act interested by asking questions. Most people love to talk about themselves, if given the chance. When you ask a question, you give them this chance. Try basic stuff like "What did you think of that movie?" or "What kind of sports do you like?"

 That's *act interested,* not *be nosy.* Avoid questions like "What did your sister do to her HAIR?" "How much did your family PAY for that?" "Granddad, you're really OLD, aren't you?"

2. Listen to the answers. People will know you're listening when you look them in the eye and nod your head every so often. Try not to space out or spend the whole time thinking of what you want to say next.

3. Make comments or ask follow-up questions. Simple statements like "Wow" or "Cool" show you're paying attention. So do questions like "You're into basketball? Which team is your favorite?"

4. Share something about yourself. Talk about your family, your interests, a book you're reading, your hobby, your pet, anything. Try to pick something you think the other person will want to hear about.

Sharing: "I'm building a model car with my Dad. It's so fun. Do you want to see it sometime?"

Bragging (ick): "I've read more books than anyone in my grade. I'm way advanced. You're probably not as smart as me."

Boring (Zzzzzz): "The naked mole rat lives its entire life in dark, underground burrows . . ."

5. Watch to see how your listeners react. Do they seem bored? Do you have to chase them around going "Dudes, I'm not finished, wait 'til you hear *this* part"? If you don't have someone's attention, politely put on the brakes.

Like this:

Whoa, I'm talking too much. Want to shoot some hoops?

Enough about me. Tell me more about the movie you went to.

I'm blabbing. Let's change the subject.

If someone's boring *you,* you can help that person switch gears. Try:

Sounds like you're really into that. Guess what? I heard this funny joke—it goes like this....

> That's interesting...
> say, should we go get
> something to eat?

> Cool. Oh, hey, I've
> been meaning to tell
> you about this new
> CD I got.

If the person is really stuck on one topic, you might have to be honest (yet polite):

> Do you mind if we talk
> about something else?

> Sorry to change
> the subject, but....

How do you end a conversation? Don't just turn your back on the person and walk away. Politely say:

> Well, it's been good talking to you.
> I have to take off now. See you later.

Clue 4 U Try to avoid junk words. Like, you know, *like* and *you know*. You know?

A Few Choice Words About Swearing*

Using swear words won't make you seem cool and grown up, just rude 'n' crude. If your friends or family members cuss, it doesn't mean you should, too.

However, there are times when you need to say *something* or you might actually explode. Maybe you're totally surprised or shocked or excited. Try using one of these mild-mannered alternatives to cuss words. Who knows, you might start a trend.

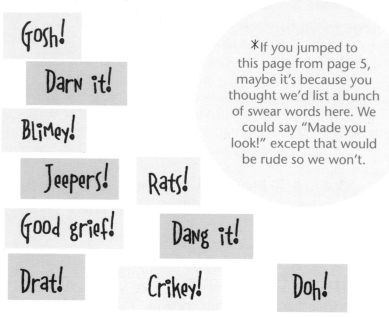

Gosh!

Darn it!

Blimey!

Jeepers!   Rats!

Good grief!   Dang it!

Drat!   Crikey!   Doh!

*If you jumped to this page from page 5, maybe it's because you thought we'd list a bunch of swear words here. We could say "Made you look!" except that would be rude so we won't.

Conversation Killers

Meet the Conversation Killers: *The Interrupter, The Complainer, The Gossiper,* and *The Motormouth.*

The Interrupter:
Constantly cuts people off. Jumps right into other people's conversations.

The Complainer: Whines about everything. "Math is stupid!" "I never get to go first!" "This is so lame!"

The Gossiper: Spreads rumors and dishes dirt. Talks about people behind their backs.

Clue 4 U Gossip is risky—it can come back to haunt you. Never say anything *about* a person that you wouldn't say *to* the person.

The Motormouth: Talks-and-talks-and-doesn't-stop-talks-and-never-lets-anyone-else-get-a-word-in-and-tells-really-long-boring-stories-and-talks-really-fast-and-hardly-ever-stops-to-take-a-breath.

Blah blah blah. Blah, BLAH blah Blah blah. Blah blah blah, BLAH BLAH blah blah! Blah BLAH blah blah, BLAH BLAH blah Blah, blah.

Whenever a Conversation Killer arrives on the scene, the conversation comes to a halt. Don't let this happen. Try the *Excuse Me, But . . .* approach. Choose one of these:

- "Excuse me, but I haven't finished what I was saying."

- "Excuse me, but all this talk about math makes me want to get outside while we can. Let's go!"

- "Excuse me, but I actually like the person you're talking about. She's really nice."

- "Excuse me, but I need a little break. Can we meet up later?"

Is It Rude to Tease?

It depends on how and why you do it. There's good teasing and then the other kind—the kind that hurts or annoys people. Good teasing is meant to draw attention to someone in a positive way. Like "Try not to hurt yourself carrying all those trophies home, okay?" This kind of teasing is usually done with a sincere smile. It makes the person who's being teased feel noticed and accepted.

Sometimes, you can tease your closest friends about their unique qualities or silly things they do—as long as you're keeping it among friends. Like "When you get Tiffany laughing hard enough, she snorts like a pig!" Or "Bart, I saw you checking out your muscles when you thought no one was looking." Say it in a way that's funny, not mean. If you put your arm around your friend or follow up with, "I'm totally kidding, okay?" then you're showing that you meant no harm. If your friend is ever offended by your teasing, say you're sorry.

The phrase "just kidding" is often misused. Like: "Where'd you get those clothes, the rag bag? Just kidding." Finishing a rude statement with "just kidding" doesn't make it better.

If you're on the receiving end of teasing you don't like, you can ignore it and walk away. Or you might say, "I don't appreciate that. Cut it out." Try not to take the teasing to heart. If someone is really bugging you and won't let up, get help from a parent or teacher.

Phone-y Manners

Does any of this ring a bell?

- **Phone rings.** You answer. It's for your dad. You drop the phone and yell "*DAAAAAAD!* PHONE!!!"

- **Phone rings.** You answer. It's for your sister. She's not home. The caller asks you to please take a message, and you say you will. The caller tells you the number for your sister to call, thinking you're writing it down. You're not. Later, you tell your sister, "You got a call. Some guy. I forgot the number."

- **Phone rings.** You answer. It's a telemarketer. You slam the phone down.

- **Phone rings.** You answer. It's for your mom. She's not home. The caller waits for you to ask, "May I please take a message?" You sit there silently, inspecting your fingernails. The person says, "Can I leave a message?" You say, "Let me get a pen" and go off to find one. After a while, the caller hangs up.

- **You're the caller.** As soon as your friend answers, you say, "*Whassup?*" Your friend pauses, then asks, "Who *is* this?"

- **You're the caller.** When a person answers "Hello?" you go, "Who's this?" There's a stern silence. Then the person says, "Who's *this?*" You get embarrassed and hang up.

- **You're the caller.** You dial a random number and someone answers. You say, "Hello, I'd like speak to Seymour Butts." The person sounds confused and says, "There's no one here by that name." You go, "*What?* I really wanna see more butts!" Then you laugh like a hyena and hang up.

Time to learn the do's and don'ts of polite phoning.

Do answer the phone with a pleasant "Hello." Don't go "*Yel*-low," "Yo," or "Yep?"

Do say "Can you hold on a moment, please?" if the call isn't for you. Set the phone down gently and go find the person the caller wants to speak to. Or place your hand over the receiver so you can tell someone that he or she has a phone call, *without the caller hearing everything you say.* Don't drop the receiver with a huge thunk or yell at someone to "COME GET THE PHONE!!"

Do keep a pad of paper and a pen by the phone. Ask, "May I please take a message?" Get the proper spelling of the person's name and the phone number with the area code. Don't assume that you can remember the name and number in your head, or write the message so sloppily that even you can't read it.

Do let telemarketers know that your family would like them to stop calling. Say, "Please take this number off your call list." Don't treat telemarketers rudely because "they deserve it."

Do choose a good time to call people. Don't call during dinner or after most people have gone to bed. And if it's 6 AM on Saturday and you're calling your friend to play, *it's too early.*

Do let the person you're calling know who you are. ("Hi, this is Petey.") Don't assume that Caller ID will do the job for you. Not everyone has Caller ID.

Do ask politely for the person you're calling. ("May I please speak to D.J.?") Don't go, "Dude, get me D.J., wouldja?"

Do use the Call Waiting feature with care. If a call comes in while you're already on the line, ask if you may put the person you're speaking to on hold—then *briefly* talk to the new caller. Don't keep people hanging. They don't have all day to wait while you take every other call that comes through.

Clue4U If a call for a parent comes in while you're talking with a friend, tell your friend you'll call back later. This shows respect and may earn you more phone privileges.

Do use Three-Way Calling in a friendly way. Everyone who's on the line should know exactly *who else* is on the line. Don't use Three-Way Calling as a trap. It's rude and mean to get Caller #2 to say something nasty about Caller #3, who just happens to be *listening in.*

HOWDY!

Sorry, Wrong Number

Kids can get flustered by wrong numbers. So you don't, here's what to do and say.

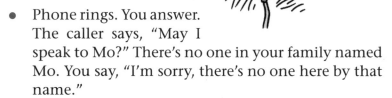

- Phone rings. You answer. The caller says, "May I speak to Mo?" There's no one in your family named Mo. You say, "I'm sorry, there's no one here by that name."

Sometimes the caller will just hang up. And sometimes the caller will ask, "What number is this?" *It's better not to say your number.* Instead, ask, "What number did you dial?" The caller should tell you.

If it's *not* your number, say, "I'm sorry, but you must have dialed wrong." If it *is* your number, say, "That's our number, but there's no one here by that name."

- You're calling your friend D.J. His number is 555-1234. You know it's the right number because you've called him a million times. When a person answers "Hello?" you say, "May I please speak to D.J.?" The person says, "There's no one here by that name."

Because you're polite, you don't just hang up. Instead, you say, "I'm sorry. I think I have the wrong number. Is this 555-1234?" The person says, "No, it's not." You say "Thank you," hang up, and dial again, this time more carefully.

Phone Safety

Your family might have its own rules about phone safety when you're home alone. If you haven't already done this, talk with your parents to learn what they want you to do.

Here are some rules other families use. Maybe your family will want to try them.

1. Never tell a caller you're home alone. Say "Mom and Dad are busy right now. May I take a message?"

2. Use Caller ID to screen calls. Only answer if the name and number that come up are familiar to you.

3. If a stranger calls and starts asking questions, hang up. That's not being rude. It's being smart. Write down the time of the call and anything you remember about it. Then tell your parents about it when they get home.

4. If a stranger calls and starts saying weird things or using bad words, hang up. Write down the time of the call and what the caller said. Tell your parents about it right away.

Cellphone Manners

Too bad cellphones don't come with manners manuals. If they did, maybe there wouldn't be so many rude cellphone users in the world. So you won't be one of them, here's a mini-manual of cellphone manners you need to know.

- Learn how your cellphone works so you can turn it off and on, adjust the ringtone volume, and set the ringer to vibrate.

- Use your regular voice. A lot of people talk MuCH MORE LOUDLY on their cellphones than they need to.

- Remember that the people around you don't need to know all the details of your life.

- Just because you *can* bring your cellphone into the bathroom doesn't mean you *should.* Nobody wants to hear you pee. Plus you could drop your phone in the toilet.

- Turn off your phone in movie theaters, libraries, restaurants, classrooms, houses of worship, and other public places.

- Try not to keep other people waiting while you talk on the phone.

- Don't interrupt a face-to-face conversation to answer your phone. *The person you're with is more important than the person who's calling.* The only exceptions to this rule are Mom and Dad.

- If your phone has a camera, never take someone's picture without his or her permission.

- If your parents are paying for your cellphone, it's rude to run up a giant-sized bill. Know how many minutes you can use each month, and keep track. If you go over, offer to pay the difference, even if it takes several months' worth of your allowance.

Class-y Manners

Want to get ahead in school? Easy: Use your manners.

You probably know this, but teachers look at more than your homework and tests. Teachers notice your behavior in class. They can't play favorites, but they *can* appreciate students who:

- Look interested

- Sit up at their desks instead of slumping and slouching

- Listen and pay attention

- Raise their hands and wait to be called on

- Do their homework and assignments

- Are neat and clean (desk, cubby, locker—and personal appearance)

- Are ready to learn (pencils sharpened, notebooks out)

- Stand in line without pushing and shoving

- Wait until after class to talk to friends

- Bring presents for the teacher every day*

  * Kidding!

We can't promise you'll get straight A's if you use manners in school. But we can tell you that students who do everything just mentioned *stand out*. They get noticed because they seem to care about themselves and others. They even appear to enjoy school. Even if your grades are only so-so, your A+ manners could lead to a better report card.

Stupid Student Tricks

Ever since the first cave-student used a slingshot to lob a giant spitball at his cave-teacher, students have been pulling pranks in class, like:

- Making rude faces behind the teacher's back

- Shooting rubber bands

- Folding paper into footballs to flick at their friends

- Tipping their chairs *waaaay* back

- Farting, burping, hiccupping, or yawning as loudly as possible

Do you play stupid student tricks? There are better ways to get attention. (Look back at the list on page 92.)

If another student tries to distract the class, what can you do? Ignore the person and go back to being the polite student you are. If the teacher isn't aware of what's going on, talk to him or her privately after class.

Recess Rudeness

Have you noticed that manners often disappear during recess? True, recess is free time—but you're not free to swear, fight, tease, push, hog the playground equipment, and boss people around.

If you have a lot of pent-up energy, find positive ways to let it out. Run, throw a ball, kick a ball, hang from the monkey bars, do cartwheels, race, shout, swing, jump rope, or organize a group game.

E-Tiquette:
Manners Online

You're at a party. A few new kids are there. One of them says something lame. Do you yell:

THAT'S SO DUMB, U-R AN IDIOT AND EVERYONE SHOULD HATE YOU

Probably not—unless you're chatting online.

For some strange reason, certain people think it's okay to act like rudeniks if they do it on a keyboard. They SHOUT (USE ALL CAPITAL LETTERS) and start flame wars (write angry emails or messages). They talk trash (badmouth people) and swear (#$%^&*!!).

But typing instead of talking doesn't make rudeness right. If you want to be a good online citizen *(netizen)*, you need to use online etiquette *(netiquette)*. If you don't, you're just a knucklehead *(nucklehead)*.

Safety First

- Never give out personal information in an email or online. This includes your address, telephone number, the name of the school you go to, your team number, or where your parents work. Don't give out anyone else's personal information, either.

- Never agree to meet someone in person you've met online before checking with your parents first. A parent should go with you, and the meeting should be in a public place.

- Never send anyone your picture before checking with your parents first.

- Never share your password with anyone, not even your best friend.

- If anything you see or read makes you feel funny or uncomfortable, tell a parent right away.

Email Manners

Be polite when you write. Start your email with a greeting. Try "Hello," "Hi," "Dear," or "Hey." (It's like saying "Hello" when you answer the phone.) End your email with a sign-off. Maybe "Sincerely," "Bye for now," "Peace," or "Best." (It's like saying "Goodbye" before you hang up the phone.)

Use a spellchecker program. Emails full of spelling mistakes are annnoyyinnng. Read your email from start to finish before you press SEND. Does it say what you mean? How do you think the other person will feel after reading it?

Avoid sending email when you're angry. Wait 24 hours. Give yourself time to cool down. Sending an angry email usually makes things worse, not better.

Don't forward chain emails or jokes (okay, maybe a few jokes). The same goes for emails that have this in the subject line:

FW: Fwd: RE: Fwd: RE: Fwd fwd RE RE: Fwd re fwd:

or look like this:

>>>>>>>>>> Why did
>>>>>>>>>> the chicken
>>>>>>>>>> cross
>>>>>>>>>> the road?

What if an email says "Forward this to everyone you know"? That email is not the boss of you. Plus it's probably a hoax—something meant to trick you into believing or doing something dumb.

Clue4U Want to know if the Two-Striped Telamonia Spider is hiding under toilet seats in public bathrooms, waiting to bite your butt? Check www.snopes.com. It's a Web site that specializes in uncovering hoaxes. Go there anytime you wonder if an email is the real thing or just a silly rumor.

Do try to answer email as soon as you can. But don't expect other people to respond to your email immediately. Maybe they're busy doing something else, like their homework.

Respect people's privacy. Never forward or post an email someone sends to you without getting that person's permission first. Never sneak a peek at someone else's email.

IM-ing

Instant messaging—online chatting—is a cool way to stay in touch with friends. You can chat with one person at a time or several people in different chat windows. You can even chat with a bunch of people in the same window.

Learn how to use your instant message program. If you're going to be away from your computer for a while, set your status to "Away." Then people won't think you're ignoring them if they IM you and you don't answer.

It's polite to give a greeting ("Hello," "Hi," "Hey there") when you start a conversation. Ask if the person has time to chat. If you're chatting and you need to leave your computer for a while, don't just disappear. Say "Be right back" or "Back in a few." When you want to end a chat, say "Gotta run!" or "Later!"

Even though an online chat feels private, it isn't. Your words show up on the other person's computer. Anyone who walks by can read them. So be careful what you write.

Chat Rooms

Creeps and criminals love chat rooms. They can pretend to be nice people and trick kids into giving them personal information.

Before you visit a chat room, have a parent or another adult you trust check it out.

Chat rooms safe for kids are *monitored*. There is always an adult watching over the chat. Also, they have a *privacy policy* that explains how your information will be protected.

Look for chat rooms you like on topics that interest you. Don't crash a chat just for fun. Keep your chats polite. Try not to insult other people. If someone insults you, stay calm. Ignore the person or send a message asking what the person meant. Maybe it was all a misunderstanding.

Clue4U To get a list of chat rooms for kids and teens, go to yahooligans.yahoo.com and do a search for **chat.**

Texting

Texting (or TXTing) on your cellphone is a great way to stay in touch. Reading and writing text messages doesn't make any noise. So you can text in places where you can't talk, like a library. Plus other people can't hear what you're saying, since you're not talking out loud.

Clue 4 U Texting in a dark room—like a movie theater—can bother the people around you. The bright screen is a big distraction. On the other hand, if you ever find yourself in a dark room and need a flashlight, you can use your cellphone.

When you text, use common courtesy—just like in email, IMs, and chat rooms. Keep your messages short and check your spelling. Don't use all caps. If you use abbreviations, make sure the person you're texting understands them.

Most cellphones beep or ring when messages come in, so don't text too early or too late in the day. If you're in a quiet place and you're expecting a text message, turn off the ringer on your cellphone. You can still check to see if a message has come in, but you won't bother anyone.

Texting when you're talking face-to-face with some-one else is rood, dood.

Clue4U Remember that anything you send over the Internet can be copied, forwarded, and stored. Plus *you can't take it back.* So don't say it if you might be sorry later. And don't say it if you wouldn't want certain other people to see it, like your parents, teachers, friends, or the police.

Public Manners

So many places to go, so many chances to act up! But that's no good. Here's how to put your best foot forward wherever you are.

Playing Sports

No bragging if you win or whining if you lose. Shake hands with the other player(s) or team. Say "Good game!" or "Nice work!" If you're really upset, calm yourself down. Slowly count to 10 or take deep breaths.

Watching Sports

Stand up for the national anthem. Take off your hat, face the flag, and put your hand over your heart.

Yeah, you love your team and you want them to win. But that doesn't mean you should trash-talk the other team or shout rude words at their fans. And if you just *have* to wear a giant foam finger, try not to block everyone's view of the game.

After You

Not *you*, silly. Other people. Hold the door for the person behind you. Let people out of an elevator, bus, or train before you go in.

Revolving Doors

Walk, don't run through revolving doors. Go around just enough to get to the other side. You are not on a merry-go-round.

Buses, Trains, Subways

Stay to the right. If you wear a backpack, remember that it makes your body about twice its normal size. Be careful when you turn around or pass someone.

Unless there are many empty seats on a bus or train, hold your belongings in your lap or slide them under your seat. Don't put them on the seat next to you.

Give up your seat for someone who needs it more than you do. You know—a man or woman holding a baby, a pregnant woman, a senior citizen, or someone who is disabled or looks really tired. Stand up, catch the person's eye, and say, "Here, you can have my seat."

Escalators, Moving Walkways

Stay to the right. Pass on the left. Don't announce "Comin' through!" and push past everyone like a thug.

Movies, Concerts, Plays, Performances

- Arrive in time to take your seat without crawling over other people. If you do have to pass other people, say "Excuse me." If you step on someone's foot, say "I'm sorry!"

- If you're wearing a hat, take it off.

- If you're at a performance where eating is allowed, munch and sip quietly. Don't pelt people with popcorn. Try to open boxes and unwrap hard candy before the performance starts, or during parts with loud music or explosions. If eating is not allowed, don't sneak in food or drinks.

Clue4U Feets don't belong on seats. That goes for movie theaters, stadiums, buses, airports, restaurants, concert halls, and anywhere else you plop down.

- Wait to talk until after the performance or during intermission.

- Avoid kicking the person's seat in front of you.

- If you have to go to the bathroom, try to wait for a good moment, like the end of a piece of music or a boring part of a movie or play. Quietly say "Excuse me" to the people you squeeze by.

- Turn off your cellphone or set the ringer to vibrate.

In the Car

The polite passenger always:

- Buckles up

- Lets the person who called "Shotgun!" first sit up front

- Talks at a normal volume

- Gives other people turns choosing radio stations or CDs to listen to

- Picks up backseat litter (food wrappers, empty bottles)

- Thanks the driver for the ride

THE WHEELS ON THE BUS GO ROUND AND ROUND! ROUND AND ROUND LA LA LA LA !....

P.S.

Adults hate it when kids fight in the backseat. Pretend there's an invisible **forcefield** between you and the other passengers. Keep your hands and other body parts to yourself at all times. Bring along headphones or a book so you can tune out.

At the Mall

Thank the store clerks, food servers, and others who help you.

Put things back where you found them. Workers spend a lot of time arranging displays and straightening shelves and bins. If you can't figure out how to re-fold a T-shirt or a pair of pants before you replace it, give it to the clerk.

Don't leave a mess in the dressing room. Put clothes back on hangers instead of piling them on the floor.

If you're with a group of friends, leave room for people to pass or go the other way.

Even though you're excited to be at the mall, keep your voice down. Watch your language. If you're people-watching, don't laugh at other people or make rude gestures behind their backs.

When Mall Workers Are Rude

You're looking at jeans when a clerk gives you the evil eye. Or the server at a restaurant treats you like dirt. Or you ask a question and the person totally ignores you.

Some workers don't trust kids because they've seen them shoplift, break stuff, or trash things. Some don't like kids. And some are just plain rude.

You can't change them. You *can* choose to shop somewhere else. Most malls have plenty of stores. Go to ones where workers appreciate polite, well-behaved kids like you.

Places of Worship

If you and your family attend a church, synagogue, or mosque, you probably know how to behave. If you go with a friend, it might be new to you.

You want to be respectful and not embarrass yourself or your friend. Dress in a quiet, modest way. Girls, wear a shirt with long sleeves and a skirt that falls below your knee. Bring a scarf in case you need to cover your head. Boys, wear a shirt with long sleeves and long pants. You may need to remove your hat or wear a special head covering.

During the service, *watch what other people do.* Follow the example of your friend and his or her family. If you're confused or not sure how to act, ask your friend.

Out and About

If you're on wheels, look out for walkers. Avoid running over people with your bicycle, skateboard, or scooter.

Don't be a litterbug. True, there are people whose job it is to pick up litter and trash. But it's rude to make them work even harder.

Walking your dog? Be sure to scoop the poop.

Memorize the next page, do what it says, and you'll be a manners **whiz.**

10 Steps to Amazing Manners Anytime, Anywhere

1. Treat others as you want to be treated.

2. Put other people first.

3. Show respect for yourself and others.

4. Be kind, be cheerful, and use common sense.

5. Share and be fair.

6. Be patient. Wait your turn.

7. Show appreciation.

8. Be a good sport.

9. Clean up after yourself.

10. Accept differences.

Be kind to animals, too.

Index

About the Authors

Pamela Espeland and Elizabeth Verdick have written many books for children and teens. They both live in Minnesota with their families and pets. They went to the same college, but not at the same time.

Other Great Books from Free Spirit

GET ORGANIZED WITHOUT LOSING IT
by Janet S. Fox

Kids learn to conquer clutter, handle homework, prepare for tests, plan projects, stop procrastinating, and enjoy the benefits of being organized: less stress and more success.

$8.95, 112 pp., B&W illust., S/C, 5⅛" x 7". Ages 8–13.

HOW TO TAKE THE GRRRR OUT OF ANGER
by Elizabeth Verdick and Marjorie Lisovskis

A hot temper isn't cool. Knowing how to manage your anger feels grrrreat. Through tips, jokes, facts, and cartoons, this book helps kids understand anger and handle it in healthy, positive ways.

$8.95, 128 pp., B&W illust., S/C, 5⅛" x 7". Ages 8–13.

BULLIES ARE A PAIN IN THE BRAIN
written and illustrated by Trevor Romain

No one wants to be picked on, pushed around, threatened, or teased. Practical suggestions and humor help kids become bully-proof, stop bullies from hurting others, and know what to do in dangerous situations.

$8.95, 112 pp., B&W illust., S/C, 5⅛" x 7". Ages 8–13.

CLIQUES, PHONIES, & OTHER BALONEY
written and illustrated by Trevor Romain

If you're on the outside, you're treated like dirt. If you're on the inside, you have to follow the rules. Who needs more rules? This book helps kids deal with cliques and learn how to make real friends.

$8.95, 136 pp., B&W illust., S/C, 5⅛" x 7". Ages 8–13.

Fast, Friendly, and Easy to Use
www.freespirit.com

Browse the catalog

Info & extras

Many ways to search

Quick check-out

Stop in and see!

1.800.735.7323 • fax 612.337.5050 • help4kids@freespirit.com